8100

WITHDRAWN

WITHDRAWN

THE LIBRARY OF WHY?™

Why Does It Rain?

Marian B. Jacobs, Ph.D.

The Rosen Publishing Group's
PowerKids Press™
New York

For my grandsons, Carlos and Gianni

Published in 1999 by The Rosen Publishing Group, Inc.
29 East 21st Street, New York, NY 10010

First Edition

Book Design: Danielle Primiceri

Photo Credits: Cover © Peter Gridley 1989/FPG International; pp. 4, 7, 8, 15, 20, 22 © 1996 PhotoDisc, Inc.; p. 11 © 1994 Image Club Graphics, Inc.; p. 12 © Mimi Cotter/International Stock; p. 16 © Chad Ehlers/International Stock; p. 19 © 1997 Digital Vision Ltd.

Jacobs, Marian B.
    Why does it rain? / by Marian B. Jacobs.
        p.   cm. — (The Library of why?)
    Includes index.
    Summary: Provides answers to such questions about the weather as "What is the atmosphere?", "How does water get into the clouds?", "What makes lightning happen?", and "What is the water cycle?"
    ISBN 0-8239-5273-8
    1. Rain and rainfall—Juvenile literature. 2. Meteorology—Juvenile literature. [1. Rain and rainfall—Miscellanea. 2. Meteorology—Miscellanea. 3. Questions and answers] I. Title. II. Series
QC924.7.J33   1998
551.57—dc21
                                                    97-48446
                                                      CIP
                                                        AC

Manufactured in the United States of America

Contents

Where Does Weather Happen?

Rain is important to the plants, animals, and people on Earth. We need rain so flowers and trees can grow and people and animals can drink. Where does rain come from? It comes from our **atmosphere** (AT-mus-feer).

The atmosphere is a layer of air that surrounds Earth. It's made up of different gases, water **vapor** (VAY-per), and dust **particles** (PAR-tih-kulz). Scientists say that no other planet in our **solar system** (SOH-ler SIS-tem) has an atmosphere. All of Earth's weather occurs within the atmosphere.

◀ *We would have no snow, rain, trees, flowers, or animals without Earth's atmosphere.*

Why Is the Sun a Weather-Maker?

All weather on Earth is made by energy from the sun. The sun is the star in the center of our solar system. Like all stars, the sun is a fiery ball of hot gases that **radiates** (RAY-dee-ayts) heat, light, and other energy. A small part of this energy reaches Earth as strong rays of sunlight. They shine through the atmosphere and warm the air and Earth. This causes temperature changes, rainy weather, and air movement, which we call wind.

The sun affects all the weather on Earth. ▶

How Does Water Get Into Clouds?

As the sun's rays heat the oceans, rivers, and lakes, some water is changed into water vapor. This is called **evaporation** (ee-VAP-uh-RAY-shun).

The sun's rays also heat the air. Warm air carries the invisible water vapor high into the sky. As the water vapor rises, it reaches the higher, cooler parts of the atmosphere. The water vapor cools and forms tiny water droplets. This is called **condensation** (kon-den-SAY-shun). When enough tiny droplets come together, they form clouds that we can see.

◀ *Some of the water in this lake will soon become part of a cloud.*

Do All Clouds Make Rain?

When water droplets **condense** (kon-DENS) to form a cloud, they condense around dust particles in the atmosphere. The particles come from sand in the deserts, ash from volcanoes, and salt from the oceans.

No two clouds are the same because they form at different heights and temperatures. And not all clouds produce rain. This is because clouds are always changing. The water they carry changes back and forth many times from vapor to liquid. If a cloud moves into warm air, the water droplets will evaporate and the cloud will disappear.

White, wispy clouds usually don't produce rain. But these dark clouds look as though they might. ▶

What Is the Inside of a Cloud Like?

From the outside, a cloud looks like white puffs of smoke. On the inside, it looks like a thick patch of fog. Try this experiment to see how water droplets form in a cloud: Open your mouth close to a mirror and breathe out gently. See the fog on the mirror? That is really a layer of tiny water droplets. The layer is water vapor from your breath that has condensed, just as it does in a cloud.

◀ *You can see the water vapor from your breath condense on a window or mirror.*

How Does a Cloud Make Rain?

Clouds contain tiny water droplets that are easily carried by wind. As the cloud moves, water droplets bump into each other. Sometimes they combine and form larger droplets. When these large droplets become too heavy to float in the air, they fall. As they fall, they bump into even more droplets and keep getting bigger and heavier. These are the drops that form and make rain.

Just like the droplets in the sky, droplets on a branch will collect until they are too heavy to hang on. Then they'll fall to the ground. ▶

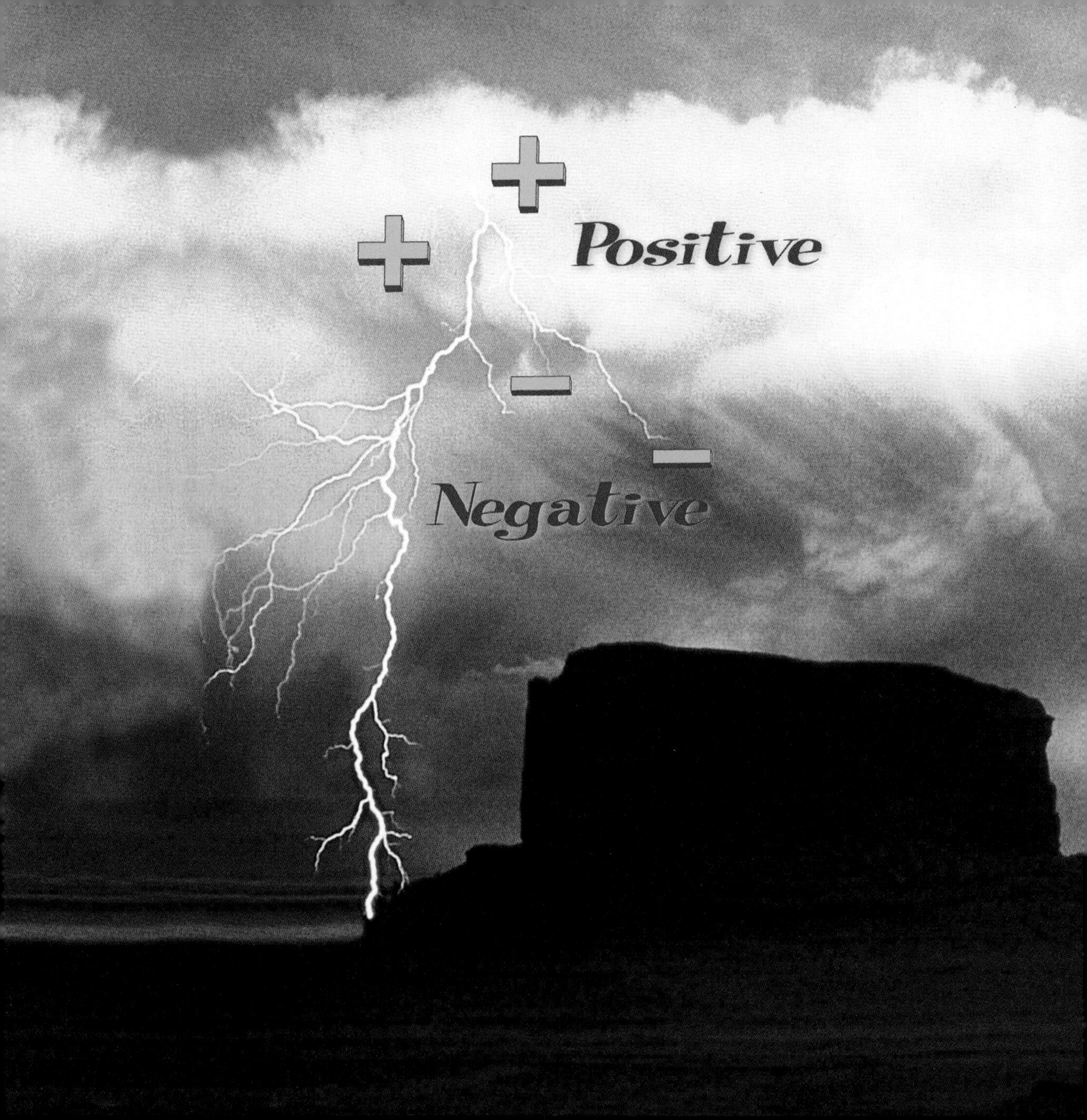
Positive
Negative

What Makes Lightning Happen?

The millions of tiny water droplets in the cloud pick up **electrical charges** (ee-LEK-trih-kul CHAR-jez). There are two kinds of electrical charges: **positive** (POZ-ih-tiv) and **negative** (NEG-uh-tiv). Water droplets with positive charges stay high up in the colder parts of the cloud. Droplets with negative charges stay lower, in the warmer parts of the cloud.

Positive and negative charges are opposites. The difference between them causes lightning to flash across the cloud.

◀ *In this picture, lightning flashes within the cloud, as well as from the cloud to the ground.*

What Makes Thunder Happen?

As lightning moves through the atmosphere, it heats and **expands** (ek-SPANDZ) the air that it passes through. This quick movement through air makes the sound that we call thunder.

The strike of lightning and the crash of thunder happen at the same time. But the light from lightning travels to your eyes faster than the sound from thunder travels to your ears. That is why you see lightning before you hear thunder.

A storm is far away when several seconds pass between the strike of lightning and the crash of thunder. A storm is close when lightning and thunder happen at almost the same time. ▶

What Makes Snow, Fog, Dew, and Frost?

Sometimes water vapor high up in the clouds gets so cold that it freezes into tiny ice crystals. These ice crystals grow into snowflakes that fall to Earth as snow.

Fog, dew, and frost don't fall from clouds. They form right where you find them. Fog is water vapor that condenses into a fine mist close to the ground. Dew forms at night on grass when water vapor in the air condenses. This is because the air near the ground is cooler than the air higher up. If the nighttime temperature is freezing, then the dew will freeze, and frost will form.

◀ *Frost is actually frozen dew.*

What Is the Water Cycle?

Water evaporates from rivers, lakes, and oceans and rises into the atmosphere as invisible water vapor. Up in the sky, water vapor cools and condenses into droplets which form clouds. Sometimes the droplets in clouds combine together and fall to the earth as rain or snow. The rain or snow enters the rivers, lakes, and oceans. Then it starts all over again. This is called the water cycle.

The total amount of water on Earth has never changed. Water just changes its form as it continues to go through the water cycle over and over again.

Glossary

atmosphere (AT-mus-feer) The layer of air, gases, and dust particles that surrounds Earth.

condensation (kon-den-SAY-shun) Cooled gas that has turned into droplets of liquid.

condense (kon-DENS) To cool and become a liquid.

electrical charge (ee-LEK-trih-kul CHARJ) Energy that can produce light, heat, or motion.

evaporation (ee-VAP-uh-RAY-shun) When a liquid is heated and then changes to a gas.

expand (ek-SPAND) To spread out.

negative (NEG-uh-tiv) A kind of electricity that is the opposite of positive.

particle (PAR-tih-kul) A very small piece of something.

positive (POZ-ih-tiv) A kind of electricity that is the opposite of negative.

radiate (RAY-dee-ayt) To spread out from something.

solar system (SOH-ler SIS-tem) A group of planets and other objects in space that circle a star.

vapor (VAY-per) A liquid that has turned into a gas.

Index